ENGINEERING
DISASTERS

THE
JOHNSTOWN
FLOOD

BY EMMA HUDDLESTON

CONTENT CONSULTANT
Carrie Davis Todd, PhD, Associate Professor of Geology,
Environmental Science Program Coordinator, Department of
Biology & Geology, Baldwin Wallace University

Core Library

An Imprint of Abdo Publishing
abdobooks.com

Cover image: An artist depicts burning debris at the
stone bridge in Johnstown, Pennsylvania.

abdobooks.com

Published by Abdo Publishing, a division of ABDO, PO Box 398166, Minneapolis, Minnesota 55439. Copyright © 2020 by Abdo Consulting Group, Inc. International copyrights reserved in all countries. No part of this book may be reproduced in any form without written permission from the publisher. Core Library™ is a trademark and logo of Abdo Publishing.

Printed in the United States of America, North Mankato, Minnesota
082019
012020

Cover Photo: Everett Historical/Shutterstock Images
Interior Photos: Everett Historical/Shutterstock Images, 1, 7, 10–11, 25, 26, 43; George W. Storm/Library of Congress, 4–5; Niday Picture Library/Alamy, 9, 22–23; Allentown Morning Call/Tribune News Service/Getty Images, 12, 45; Kean Collection/Archive Photos/Getty Images, 14–15; William H. Mullins/Science Source, 18; Bettmann/Getty Images, 21; Sheridan Libraries/Levy/Gado/Archive Photos/Getty Images, 29; Library of Congress/Corbis Historical/VCG/Getty Images, 32–33; iStockphoto, 35; Maurice Savage/Alamy, 36; Ted Spiegel/Corbis Historical/Getty Images, 39; Gal Photos/Shutterstock Images, 40

Editor: Marie Pearson
Series Designer: Ryan Gale

Library of Congress Control Number: 2019941996

Publisher's Cataloging-in-Publication Data

Names: Huddleston, Emma, author.
Title: The Johnstown flood / by Emma Huddleston
Description: Minneapolis, Minnesota : Abdo Publishing, 2020 | Series: Engineering disasters | Includes online resources and index.
Identifiers: ISBN 9781532190735 (lib. bdg.) | ISBN 9781532176586 (ebook)
Subjects: LCSH: Floods--Juvenile literature. | Pennsylvania--Johnstown (Cambria County)--Juvenile literature. | Disasters--Juvenile literature. | Engineering--Juvenile literature. | Dam safety--Juvenile literature.
Classification: DDC 974.877--dc23

CONTENTS

CHAPTER
ONE

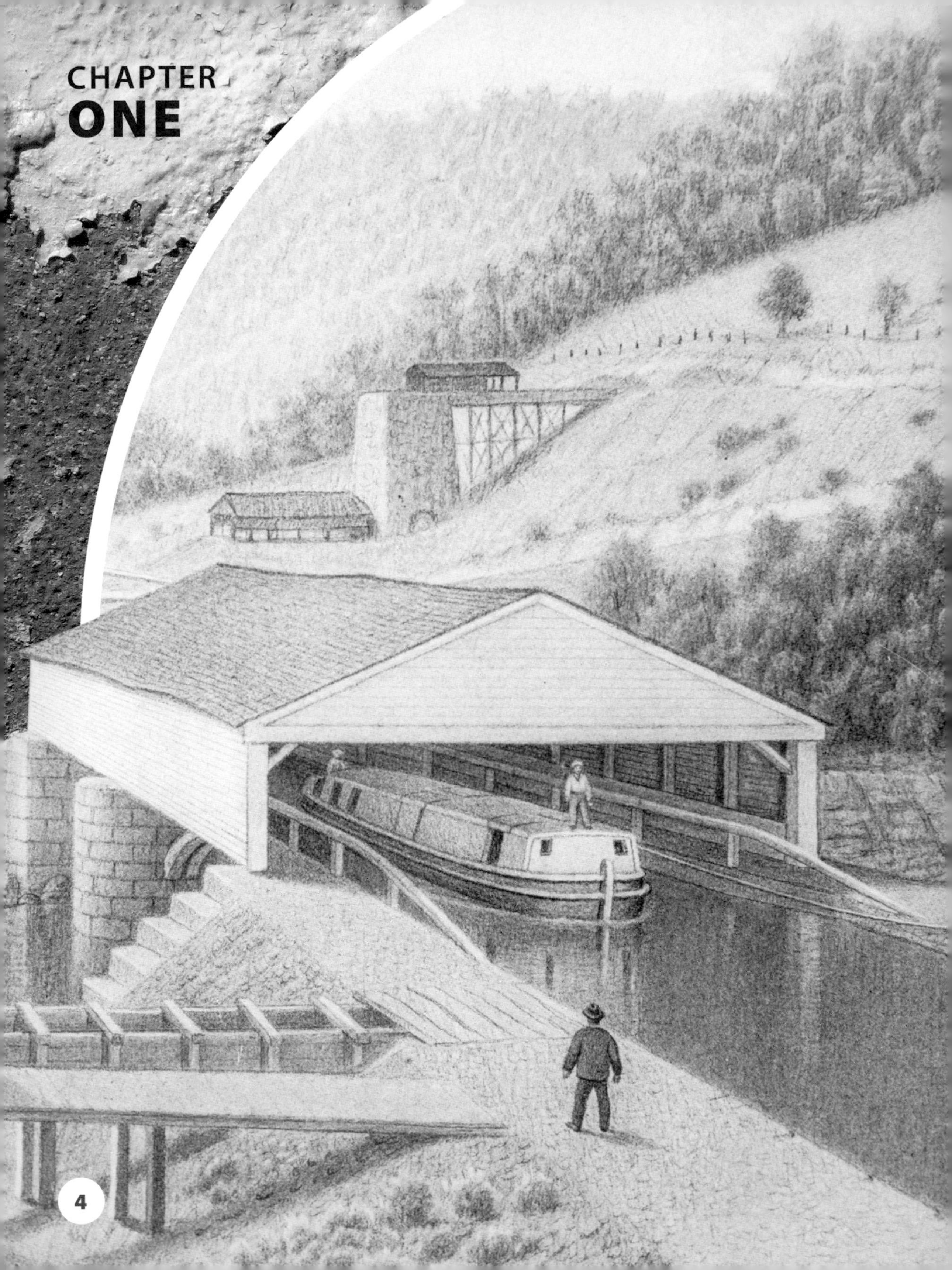

THE GREAT FLOOD OF 1889

The rain started in Pennsylvania on May 30, 1889. The Johnstown-South Fork area got 7 inches (18 cm) of rain over two days. Johnstown is a city in that area. The Little Conemaugh River runs through it. More than 30,000 people lived there. Small streams filled and flowed faster. Telegraph lines stopped working. Water rose higher. The people wondered if the river would flood.

There was a lake several miles from the town. A dam restricted how much water the lake fed the Little Conemaugh River. Suddenly, on May 31, the dam collapsed. The water rushed downhill. This journey caused the water

Johnstown had many canals for boats to travel on.

5

to gain speed. It destroyed nearly everything in its path. Trees toppled. The water carried them with it.

A wave that towered 35 feet (11 m) high hit the city. The water flowed down Main Street. It broke windows. Train cars floated off their tracks. The water picked up houses. Some people were swept away. Others climbed into their attics for safety. Water splashed off of the mountains on the far side of the city and washed back into town. The water was up to 30 feet (9 m) deep in some places.

FLOODS

A flood is a natural event where water overflows land that is normally dry. Flood water can range in depth. It can be just a few inches or it can cover a house. Flooding is the most common natural disaster in the United States. It can happen in every US state. Flooding is important for the natural world. The Nile River in Egypt floods after dry seasons. The flooding brings nutrients to the soil. This helps the plants, insects, and animals that live there.

MORE MISFORTUNE

Debris from the flood piled up at the edge of town. A bridge

The flood destroyed homes and businesses in Johnstown.

trapped it there. A few survivors were also trapped with the debris. The heap of debris covered 30 acres (12 ha). Eventually, the water drained under the bridge. It flooded nearby towns.

The water was gone, but the debris stayed. Planks of wood from buildings were scattered everywhere.

Rocks and tree branches were in the mess. People trapped in the debris called for help. Others came to their rescue. They searched the pile and pulled people out.

A few hours after the flood, a kerosene tank caught fire. The flames spread to the debris. The fire raged for three days. Eighty people died in the blaze.

THE TOLL

The Johnstown flood of 1889 is known as one

JOHNSTOWN
MAP

This map shows the path of the flood from Lake Conemaugh to Johnstown. How does this map help you understand the extent of the damage done by the flood?

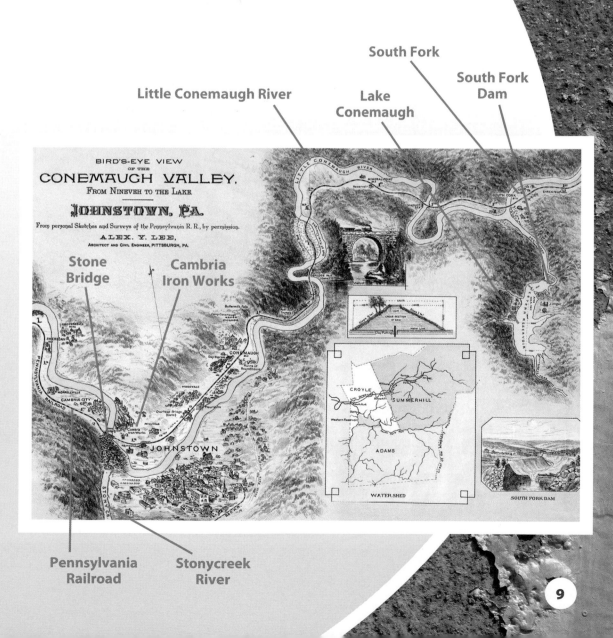

South Fork

South Fork Dam

Little Conemaugh River

Lake Conemaugh

Stone Bridge

Cambria Iron Works

Pennsylvania Railroad

Stonycreek River

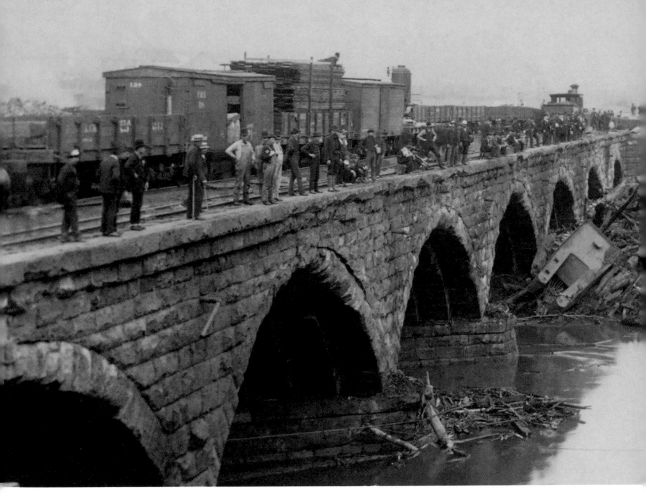

The Stone Bridge blocked debris from the flood.

of the worst floods in history. Survivors suddenly lost their homes and loved ones. More than 2,200 people died. This included 99 entire families. The exact number of deaths was impossible to count. The water carried some bodies hundreds of miles away. Some people who

died could not be recognized. They were buried in a grave called the Plot of the Unknown.

The flood caused $17 million in property damage. That was equal to approximately $473 million in 2019. It ruined 1,600 homes. The destruction led to an investigation.

The Plot of the Unknown has a monument called the Monument of Tranquility in honor of the flood victims.

People wanted to know why the flood was so massive.
They wanted to know how to avoid a similar disaster in the future.

STRAIGHT TO THE
SOURCE

Emma Ehrenfeld lived in South Fork in 1889. That was the first town hit by the flood. She was working when the flood arrived. Ehrenfeld remembered the moment of disaster:

> I then went to the window and looked out and saw people running, and some were screaming, and some [hollered] for me to come, and I looked out of the window on the side of the river, and saw [the water] coming. . . .
>
> It just seemed like a mountain coming, and it seemed close; of course, I don't know just how close it was, but I knew I must go if I wanted to get out, and I started and ran down the stairs without waiting to get my hat or anything. . . . It was a very short time, not more than two minutes until the office was taken.

Source: "Statement of Emma Ehrenfeld." *Johnstown Flood*. National Park Service, February 26, 2015. Web. Accessed April 2, 2019.

Consider Your Audience
Read this passage closely. Consider how you would adapt it for a different audience, such as your younger friends. What is the most effective way to get your point across to this audience? How does your new approach differ from the original text, and why?

CHAPTER
TWO

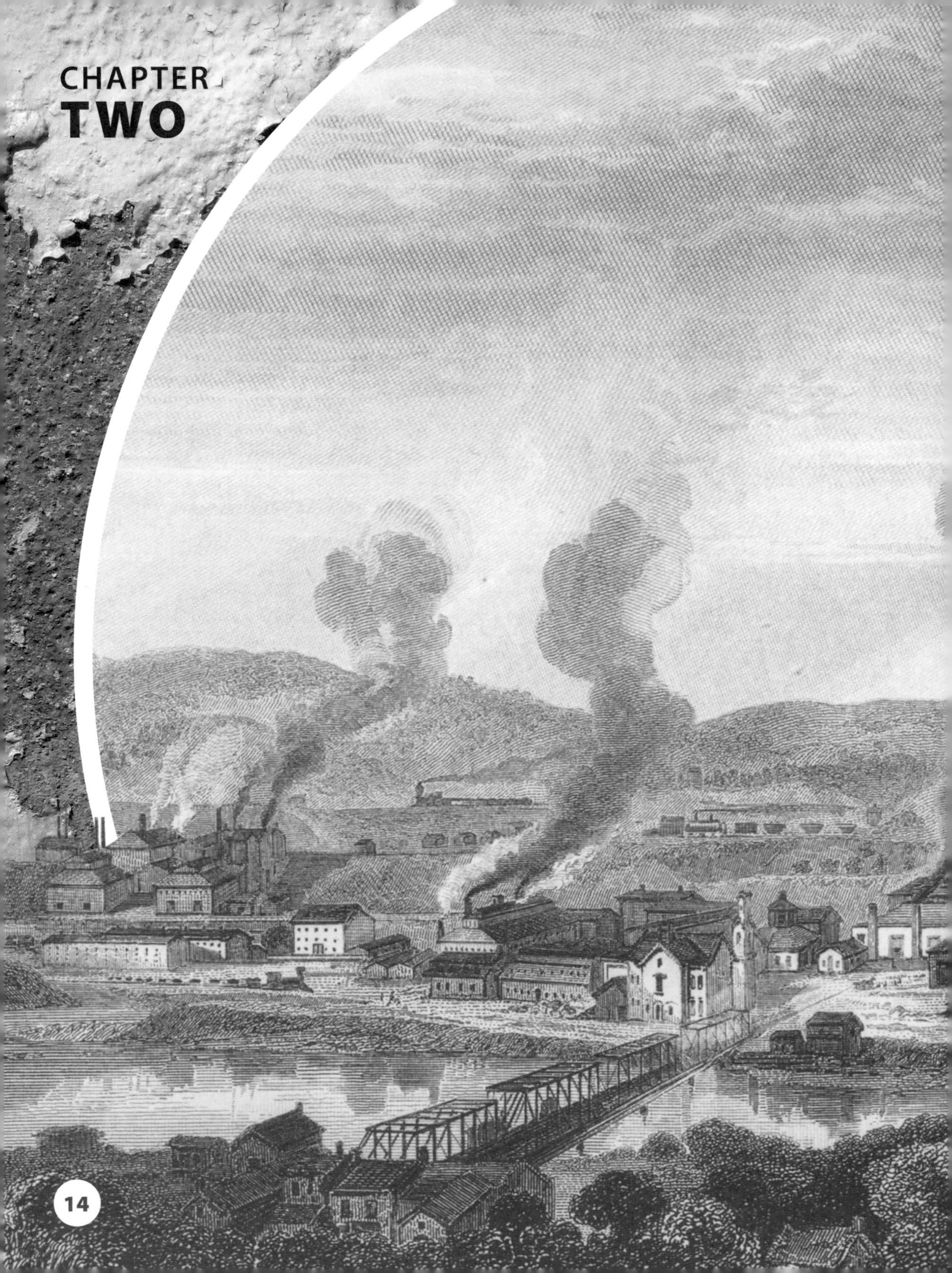

THE SOUTH FORK DAM DISASTER

Canals were an important transportation system across Pennsylvania in the 1800s. Canals are waterways that people dig. Some are built to bring water to crops. Boats travel through others.

Johnstown is in a valley of the Allegheny Mountains. It is the meeting point of the Little Conemaugh and Stonycreek Rivers. Canals helped people move goods. State leaders decided to build a dam on the south fork

Cambria Iron Works was a leader in the steel industry. Based out of Johnstown, it made steel for railroads.

of the Little Conemaugh River. The dam would help control water levels in the canals. Railroads would move boats from one canal to another.

THE SOUTH FORK DAM

The dam was built near the town of South Fork. This is 14 miles (23 km) upstream from Johnstown. The dam blocked some water from the river. This formed a reservoir. Reservoirs are lakes where water is stored. This one was named Lake Conemaugh.

The South Fork Dam was part of the canal system. It collected water and drained it slowly and safely. The lake collected water during rainy seasons. In dry seasons, a drain released water into the canal. This kept water levels steady. Boats could travel at all times of year.

Engineer William Morris designed the dam. It was 860 feet (260 m) across and 72 feet (22 m) high. The top was 40 feet (12 m) thick. On the valley floor, it was 500 feet (150 m) thick. It was possibly the largest earth dam in the world at the time. An earth dam is made of dirt and rock. Other types of dams are made of steel and concrete.

Construction began in 1840. The valley floor was cleared. This made a foundation of bare rock. Layers of clay and earth were rolled 2 feet (0.6 m) thick. They were puddled to make them waterproof. Stone called riprap covered parts of the dam. This kept it from washing away. The dam had two spillways too. These are paths dug lower than the crest, or top, of a dam. They let extra water flow out if the dam gets too full. The dam was finished in 1852.

THE RAILROAD INDUSTRY

Railroads could move large loads quickly from place to place. They connected to Johnstown in the 1850s. They replaced the use of canals. They were more convenient. Railroads needed building materials. Johnstown became known for making steel. It made the first American-made steel rails for railroads in the 1800s.

PARTS OF AN
EARTH DAM

Earth dams have many parts. Each part plays a different role in how the dam works. Choose two parts labeled in the diagram. Write what each part does. Why is this part important for the dam structure as a whole?

Dam Crest

Reservoir

Riprap

Drain

Spillway

DAM FAILURE

The dam was designed carefully. However, it was not built responsibly. Heavy rains during building washed away some materials. In 1847, this led to some flooding downstream. Some people questioned the dam's strength. Water seeped through it. In 1854, it leaked. After a heavy rain in 1856, people worried it might break.

The canal system became less important in the late 1850s. Railroads took over as the major form of transportation. The state Canal Commission sold the dam to the Pennsylvania Railroad in 1857. After that, the dam changed ownership many times. Owners neglected it. Weather damaged it. No one made proper repairs.

When the rain came in May 1889, Lake Conemaugh filled. It could not drain quickly enough. The dam failed. It released 3.8 billion gallons (14 billion L) of water. Water rushed downhill at speeds of more than 254,000 cubic feet per second (7,200 cubic m/s). The rock and soil went with it. The lake emptied in as little as 65 minutes.

EXPLORE ONLINE

Chapter Two discusses how the South Fork Dam was built. The website below talks about how and why dams are built. How is the information from the website the same as the information in Chapter Two? What new information did you learn?

BRITANNICA KIDS: DAM
abdocorelibrary.com/johnstown-flood

Lake Conemaugh drained quickly. There was little water left after the dam broke.

CHAPTER THREE

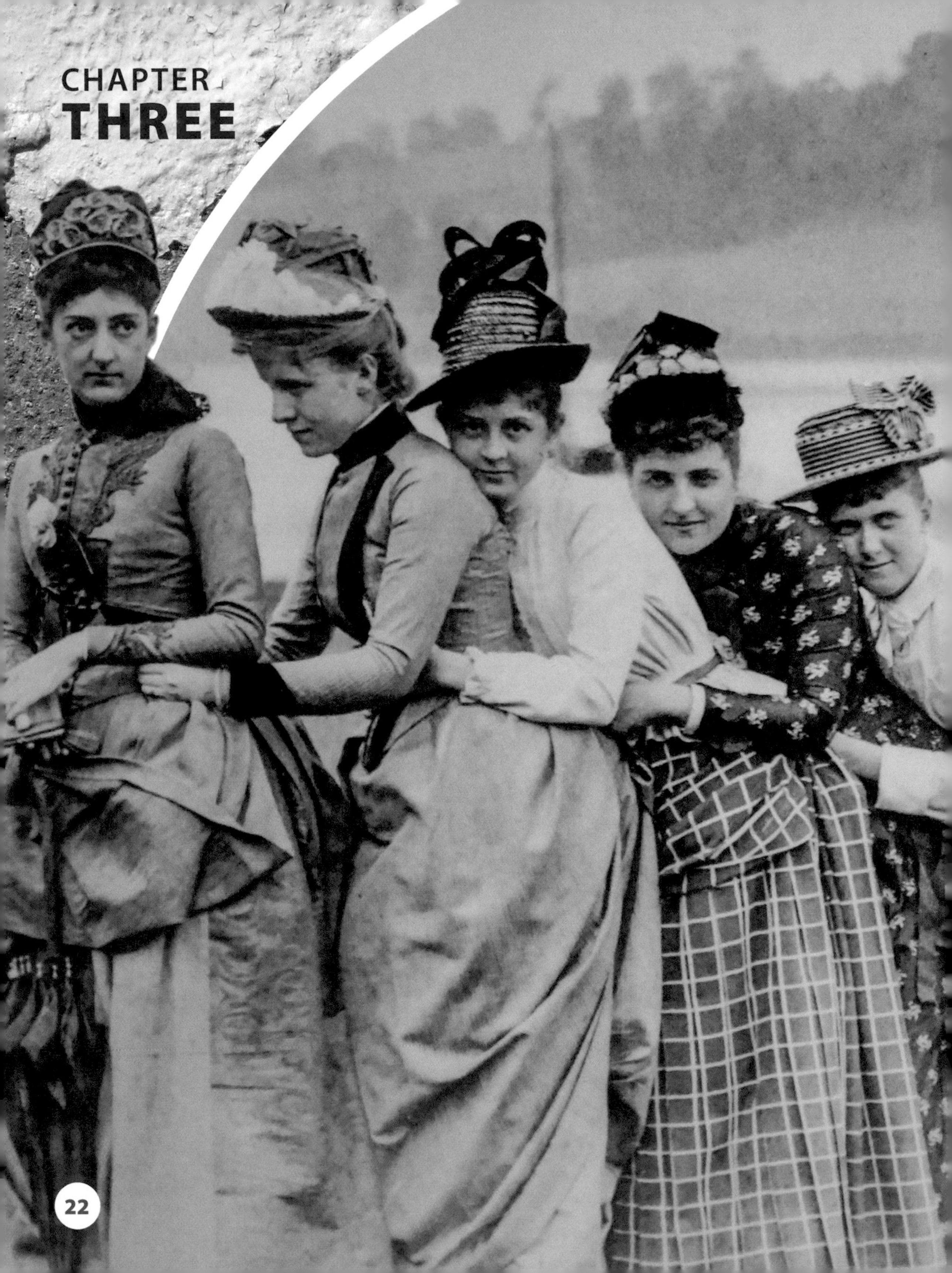

WHO WAS RESPONSIBLE?

The last owner of the dam was the South Fork Fishing and Hunting Club. Wealthy businessmen were in the club. The club turned Lake Conemaugh into a private getaway. The lake was 2 miles (3.2 km) long and 1 mile (1.6 km) wide. It was approximately 60 feet (18 meters) deep near the dam.

THE CLUB'S RISKY CHANGES

The original dam had several ways to drain the lake. Large pipes under the dam controlled water. A gate to the pipes could be opened to carry water out of the lake. When water

Businessmen often brought their families to the club. The women enjoyed socializing together.

TAKING APART THE DAM

The original riprap included large, strong stones. Over time, heavy rainfall and some leaks washed away stones near the top and middle. In 1862, people built up the riprap. But they used smaller stones. These stones were easier to wash away. In 2016, researchers from the University of Pittsburgh at Johnstown studied the design of the original South Fork Dam. They found it could survive extreme amounts of added water for 14 hours without overtopping. Its pipes could drain twice the amount of water coming into the lake.

rose high, it flowed down spillways before overflowing the dam.

By the time the club got the dam in 1880, it was in poor shape. Only one of its two spillways remained. The drain pipes were gone. A previous owner sold them. They were never replaced. This left no way to drain the lake or repair the dam. The dam also sagged in the middle. Rain and wind had washed away rock and soil.

Andrew Carnegie, a wealthy leader in the steel industry, was one member of the South Fork Fishing and Hunting Club.

The club made several changes to the dam. It bought cheap materials from local people to fill in the dam. This included hay and mud. The mud was not puddled. It could easily wash away. Water could seep through it. The club lowered the height of the dam. This made the top wider, like a road. It was easier for wagons to get to the clubhouse. The club added a mesh screen to the spillway. This kept all the fish in the lake for the club. But the screen also trapped debris, which kept water from escaping to the spillway.

These changes put the dam at risk. It could not work properly. The lake's water level rose year after year. When the rain came in 1889, people tried to act quickly. Workers frantically dug into the backup spillway. They tried to make it deeper so water could start draining. But it was too late. The workers tried to warn people downstream. However, their message may not have arrived.

INVESTIGATING THE CAUSE

The American Society of Civil Engineers investigated the disaster. Four engineers looked into whether the club's repairs made the dam weaker. They researched whether the storm was strong enough to overflow a working dam. So they looked at the original dam height and water flow. These measures would show whether the original dam could have handled the storm. The height of the dam affects how much water the reservoir can hold. The height of the crest compared to the

Many people lost everything in the flood.

EMOTIONAL POEM

A man named Isaac Reed wrote a poem after the Johnstown flood. Some lines from it read, "Many thousand human lives . . . Lovers burnt and sweethearts drowned, Darlings lost but never found! . . . Such was the price that was paid for—fish!" Reed's poem shows different emotions that many shared. People were sad about the lives lost. They were also angry with the club. Reed's poem shows two different perspectives for remembering the lake. Club members used the lake for fishing and fun. Other people who thought of the lake were reminded of death and loss.

spillway determine how quickly water can drain in emergencies.

The report stated the dam would have failed no matter what. This meant the club was not responsible. The failure was just an unfortunate natural disaster. This was good news for the club. However, this report was not shared with the public until two years after the disaster. The engineers did not want to get involved with court cases.

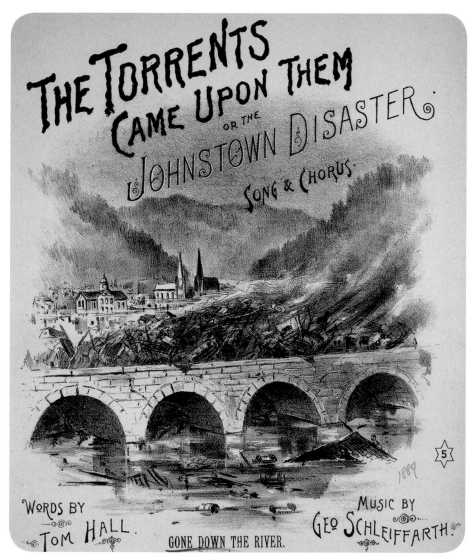

Some people composed music inspired by the flood.

CONTROVERSY THEN AND NOW

Some court cases in the 1890s tried and failed to

hold the club responsible. The engineers' report

helped the club. The club members did not have to pay for any damage. This upset people. They blamed the club for the dam failure. The dam failure ruined their homes. Some didn't have enough money to rebuild. Some people were angry that that no one was held responsible.

On the other hand, it is possible club members did not know how weak the dam was. The club may have been unaware of the danger it could cause. People today still have different opinions about how much club members knew.

The controversy about who was responsible continued. In 2016, University of Pittsburgh geologists investigated the dam failure. They stated that the changes the club made did greatly affect the dam's ability to handle major storms. One big factor was the lack of drain pipes. This 2016 report decided a properly repaired dam wouldn't have broken. It could have saved thousands of lives.

STRAIGHT TO THE
SOURCE

David McCullough wrote a history book about the Johnstown flood. He talked about his writing experience and what he learned:

> "I'd never written a book before. . . . As soon as I got into the research part of it, I knew that that was the kind of work I wanted to do from then on. . . .

> "By the time I was nearing the end, I suddenly realized what the theme is about," McCullough said. "And that is something that we must keep in mind today, as never before: that it's dangerous—perhaps even perilous—to assume that because people are in positions of responsibility they are therefore behaving responsibly. You can never assume that."

Source: Dave Sutor. "Johnstown Flood." *The (Johnstown) Tribune-Democrat*. Associated Press, March 24, 2018. Web. Accessed April 2, 2019.

Changing Minds

Take a position on whether or not leaders should take responsibility in a disaster, then imagine that your friend has the opposite opinion. Write a short essay trying to change your friend's mind. Make sure you detail your opinion and your reasons for it. Include facts and details that support your reasons.

CHAPTER
FOUR

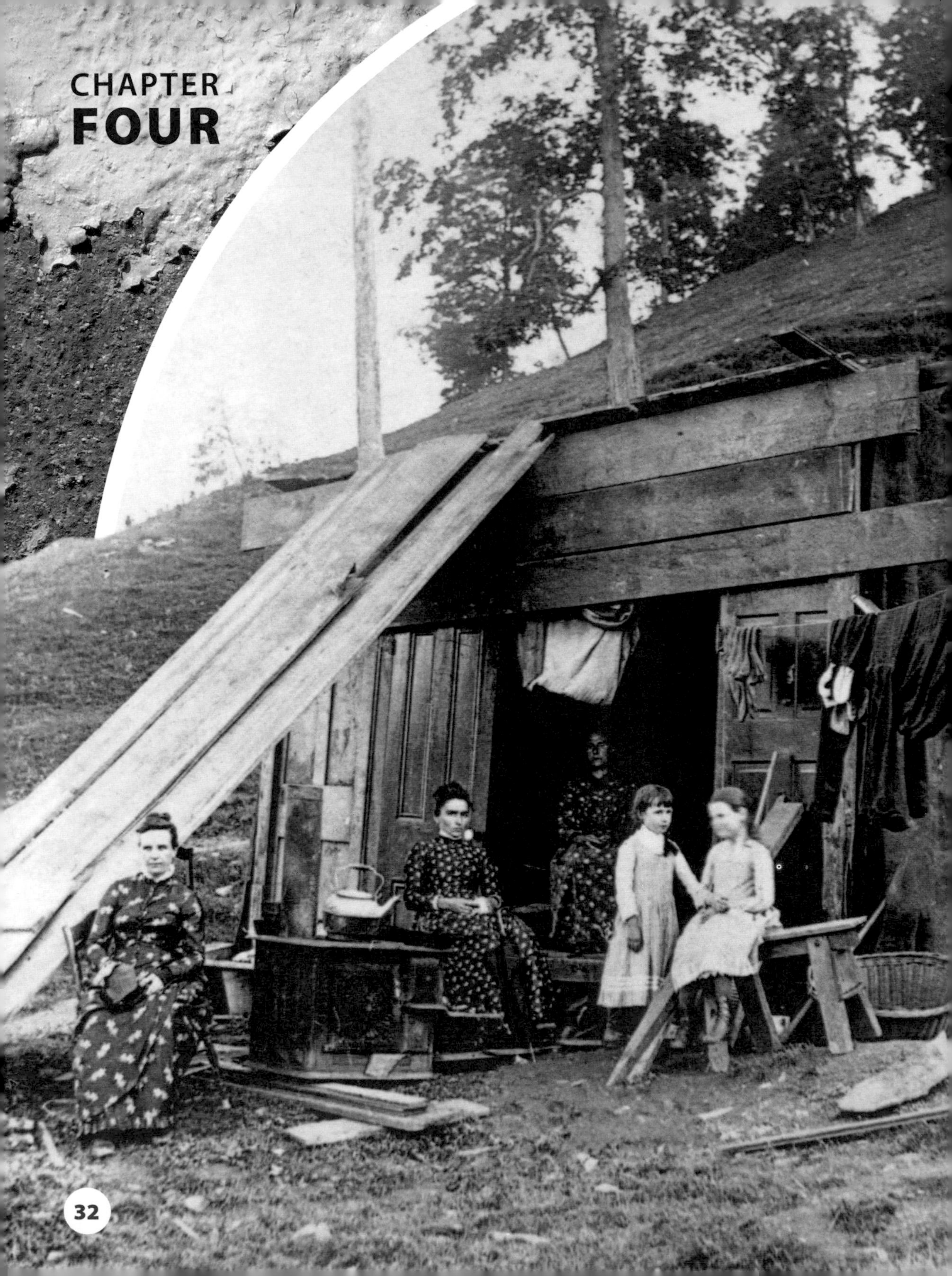

MOVING FORWARD

The American Red Cross played a big role in helping Johnstown recover. Clara Barton founded the disaster relief organization in 1881. The flood was one of the first major disasters it handled. Barton helped collect $3.7 million for the relief effort. Money came from the United States and 18 other countries. She organized thousands of volunteers. They brought food. They helped cart away debris off of Main Street. They built temporary homes.

After five years, Johnstown showed no signs of the flood. The town rebuilt

Some families had to live in temporary shelters after the flood.

33

ST. PATRICK'S DAY FLOOD OF 1936

In March 1936, Johnstown was deep in snow. It started melting. Then the rain came. By March 17, 5 to 8 inches (12–20 cm) had fallen. The snowmelt added to the rainfall. One-third of the city flooded under 17 feet (5m) of cold water. Stonycreek had 30 feet (9 m) of water. That was 15 feet (4.5 m) higher than the normal flood height. This flood did approximately $42 million in damage. It left people in Johnstown frustrated. Floods continued to be a problem.

fairly quickly. It relied on industries such as iron and steel production. Railroad construction was booming. Cambria Iron Works was the main steel producer in Johnstown. It reopened after the flood. It stayed open until 1992. It became one of the largest rail producers in the United States.

NO NEW DAM

No one rebuilt the dam. It was costly. The city didn't use the canal system any more. It didn't need to control canal levels.

People can still see old Cambria Iron Works buildings in Johnstown.

Visitors can learn more about the flood at the Johnstown Flood National Memorial.

However, Johnstown is on a floodplain. A floodplain is low-lying ground near a river. This location puts it at risk for frequent flooding. Big rainfalls and snowmelts upstream cause the river to swell.

The US Army
Corps of Engineers
studied different types
of flood protection for
Johnstown. It decided
widening the river
channels was the best
option to control flood
waters. More water
could flow in them
instead of flooding
the streets.

In 1943, the
Johnstown Local
Flood Protection
Program (JLFPP) was
finished. It cost almost
$9 million. It was the
second-largest river
improvement project

HELP FROM THE WHITE HOUSE

By the 1930s, the people
of Johnstown were tired of
floods. Another flood caused
by snowmelt struck Johnstown
in 1936. It was expensive and
exhausting to rebuild year
after year. People from the
city wanted help. They wrote
more than 15,000 letters
to President Franklin D.
Roosevelt. He responded,
"We want to keep you from
having these floods again. The
federal government, if I have
anything to do with it, will
cooperate with your state and
community to prevent further
flooding." This led to the
flood protection system built
in 1943.

in the country at the time. The river channels were dug wider and deeper. Concrete walls supported the sides of the rivers. Dirt and grass riverbeds slow waterflow. Water could flow more quickly across the walls. Ramps and stairs were built along the rivers. This made it easier for people to do repairs if needed.

In 1977, another flood struck Johnstown. But it wasn't as disastrous. The flood was caused by heavy rainfall. The flood protection system helped. Wider river channels carried flood water out of town. The flood water was 11 feet (3.4m) lower than it would have been without JLFPP. Eighty-five people died, most from smaller dams that broke. But it is likely the system kept many more people from being killed.

LAWS CHANGED

Laws have changed since the Johnstown flood. Landowners are more likely to be held responsible for damage their property causes. In the 1860s, a fabric company in the United Kingdom used a reservoir to

The 1977 flood destroyed many buildings in Johnstown.

supply water to its factory. One day, the reservoir burst. The water damaged a neighbor's property. Courts decided that the company was responsible. It didn't try to harm the neighbor. However, its poor use of land still caused damage.

Today laws and improved flood control structures help protect Johnstown from major flooding.

This case began to influence US courts at the end of the 1800s. But not all courts followed this ruling at the time of the Johnstown flood. Laws about who is responsible for damages became stricter in the 1900s. If these laws had been in place when the Johnstown flood happened, the court cases would have ended differently. Survivors would not have had to try to prove the club neglected the dam. Instead, the club would be responsible for damage.

People remember the Johnstown flood as an important part of history. Engineers investigated. They built better flood protection systems. Many people worked hard to solve the problems caused by the flood. They wanted to avoid another disaster caused by neglect.

FURTHER EVIDENCE

Chapter Four talks about how Johnstown moved forward. Identify the main point and some key supporting evidence. Look at this website. Find a quote that supports the chapter's main point. Does the quote support a piece of evidence already in the chapter? Or does it add a new piece of information?

WHAT TO DO IN A FLOOD

abdocorelibrary.com/johnstown-flood

FAST FACTS

- Johnstown is a city in Pennsylvania. On May 31, 1889, the town flooded. The South Fork Dam failed, and 3.8 billion gallons (14 billion L) of water rushed into the city.

- More than 2,200 people died. Most died from the flood. Eighty died when a pile of debris caught on fire.

- The South Fork Dam was originally built as part of the canal system across Pennsylvania. When railroads became popular, the dam and reservoir were sold off. Owners neglected to maintain and repair the dam.

- The South Fork Fishing and Hunting Club owned the dam and reservoir when it failed. Many people blame the club for the disaster. The club had made several changes that weakened the dam.

- The original investigation into the dam failure did not hold the club responsible. However, a 2016 report concluded that a properly built and maintained dam could have survived the storm.

- Johnstown rebuilt quickly after the flood. It relied on steel production for money. It also received help from the American Red Cross.

- Laws in the United States became stricter in the 1900s. People and companies were responsible for any damage their property caused, whether or not they had neglected their land.

STOP AND THINK

Tell the Tale

Chapter Four of this book discusses a court case in the United Kingdom that led to laws changing in the United States. Imagine you have the power to change a law. Write 200 words about what you would do. What law would you want to change? Why? How would you make it different?

Another View

This book talks about the impact of the Johnstown flood of 1889. As you know, every source is different. Ask a librarian or another adult to help you find another source about this event. Write a short essay comparing and contrasting the new source's point of view with that of this book's author. What is the point of view of each author? How are they similar and why? How are they different and why?

Dig Deeper

After reading this book, what questions do you still have about how dams work? With an adult's help, find a few reliable sources that can help you answer your questions. Write a paragraph about what you learned.

Say What?

Studying floods and engineering means learning a lot of new vocabulary. Find five words in this book you've never heard before. Use a dictionary to find out what they mean. Then write the meanings in your own words, and use each word in a new sentence.

GLOSSARY

canal
a waterway dug by
people for a purpose
such as watering crops or
for transportation

debris
pieces of garbage or
wreckage from a storm or
natural disaster

found
to start an organization
or business

foundation
a base that something is built
on top of

investigate
to look closely at the details
and facts of a situation

kerosene
a liquid that catches fire
easily and is often used
for fuel

neglect
to be careless or give little
attention to something

puddle
a way of rolling mud to seal it
so water can't leak through it

theme
the main point of a project
or paper

ONLINE RESOURCES

To learn more about the Johnstown flood, visit our free resource websites below.

Core Library
CONNECTION
FREE! COMMON CORE MULTIMEDIA RESOURCES

Visit **abdocorelibrary.com** or scan this QR code for free Common Core resources for teachers and students, including vetted activities, multimedia, and booklinks, for deeper subject comprehension.

Booklinks
NONFICTION NETWORK
FREE! ONLINE NONFICTION RESOURCES

Visit **abdobooklinks.com** or scan this QR code for free additional online weblinks for further learning. These links are routinely monitored and updated to provide the most current information available.

LEARN MORE

Abdo, Kenny. *How to Survive a Flood*. Minneapolis, MN: Abdo Publishing, 2019.

Jennings, Terry Catasús. *Hydroelectric Energy*. Minneapolis, MN: Abdo Publishing, 2017.

INDEX

About the Author

Emma Huddleston lives in the Twin Cities with her husband. She enjoys writing educational books, but she likes reading novels even more. When she is not writing or reading, she likes to stay active by running and swing dancing.